I AM NOT AN OLD SOCK

THE RECYCLING PROJECT BOOK

BAINTE DEN STOC

WITHDRAWN FROM DLR LIBRARIES STOCK

KU-432-923

THIS IS A CARLTON BOOK

Published in 2018 by Carlton Books Limited, an imprint of the
Carlton Publishing Group, 20 Mortimer Street, London W1T 3JW

Text and design copyright © Carlton Books Limited 2018

All rights reserved. This book is sold subject to the condition that it
may not be reproduced, stored in a retrieval system or transmitted
in any form or by any means, electronic, mechanical, photocopying,
recording or otherwise, without the publisher's prior consent.

A catalogue record for this book is available from the British Library.

ISBN: 978-1-78312-420-6

Printed in Dongguan, China

10 9 8 7 6 5 4 3 2 1

Author: Sara Stanford
Executive Editor: Stephanie Stahl
Creative Director: Clare Baggaley
Design Manager: Emily Clarke
Production Controller: Nicola Davey
Written, designed, illustrated
and packaged by: Dynamo Limited

The publishers would like to thank the following sources for their
kind permission to reproduce the pictures in this book.
Page 27: Erik Lam/Shutterstock; page 39: Susan Schmitz/Shutterstock

Every effort has been made to acknowledge correctly and
contact the source and/or copyright holder of each picture
and Carlton Books Limited apologizes for any unintentional errors
or omissions that will be corrected in future editions of this book.

I AM NOT AN OLD SOCK

THE RECYCLING PROJECT BOOK

CARLTON
KIDS

AWESOME THINGS TO MAKE WITH SOCKS!

Hi THERE!

WELCOME TO I AM NOT A SOCK. IT'S THE **AWESOME** BOOK THAT'S PACKED **FULL** WITH **EASY TO DO** CRAFTS AND ARTY **PROJECTS** FOR ALL THE **FAMILY.**

WE WILL SHOW YOU HOW TO TURN A HUMBLE SOCK INTO A SNOWMAN, A COLOURFUL OCTOPUS OR EVEN A SET OF JUGGLING BALLS, PLUS LOTS MORE! IT'S TIME TO GET CREATIVE, SO LET THE FUN BEGIN...

DÚN LAOGHAIRE-RATHDOWN LIBRARIES	
DLR27000052379	
BERTRAMS	27/10/2019
GE	02438739

YOU'LL NEED A GROWN-UP TO HELP YOU WITH ALL OF THE MAKES!

TOP TIP!
FABRIC SCISSORS WORK BEST FOR CUTTING YOUR SOCKS BUT PLEASE ALWAYS ASK A GROWN-UP TO DO THIS BIT!

YOU WILL NEED

- A VARIETY OF SOCKS IN DIFFERENT COLOURS
- COTTON WOOL
- GLUE
- TAPE
- SAFE SCISSORS – FABRIC SCISSORS WORK BEST BUT ALWAYS ASK AN ADULT
- THREAD

- STRING
- BUTTONS
- GOOGLY EYES
- RIBBON
- PENS
- COLOURFUL CARD OR PAPER
- PIPE CLEANERS
- FEATHERS

- UNCOOKED RICE – FOR FILLING YOUR SOCK CREATIONS
- SCRAPS OF MATERIAL, FABRIC, SOCKS AND COTTON WOOL FOR STUFFING
- GOOGLY EYES

CONTENTS

OCTOPUS!

I LIVE IN THE BOTTOM OF **THE OCEAN**, NOT THE BOTTOM OF THE **LAUNDRY BASKET!**

YOU WILL NEED
- ONE COLOURFUL SOCK
- WADDING
- SAFETY SCISSORS
- GLUE
- GOOGLY EYES

LET'S GO FOR A DIP!

SET THE SCENE

Paint blue and green waves onto a piece of card until there is no white remaining, then fill it with cut-out fish and exciting sea creatures. You could use tin foil to make super shiny fish and stick on little stones or shells to make a sea floor. Your octopus friends will feel right at home in this watery world.

DID YOU KNOW?
OCTOPUSES HAVE NO BONES BUT THEY DO HAVE 3 HEARTS AND 9 BRAINS!

WITH MY 8 LEGS AND COLOURFUL PATTERNS, THERE ARE NO OTHER ANIMALS ON THE PLANET LIKE ME.

GO FURTHER!

FANCY TRYING SOMETHING A LITTLE DIFFERENT? TURN OVER THE PAGE TO MAKE THESE FUNNY FACES.

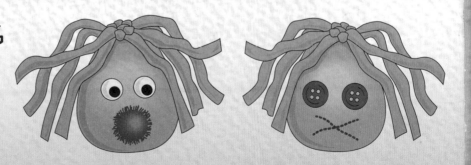

I'M AN OCTOPUS!

1

Push a handful of wadding to the toe end of your sock to make the body. It should fill up to half-way down your sock.

2

Carefully cut eight strips. Start at the open end of your sock and cut until you have almost reached the stuffing.

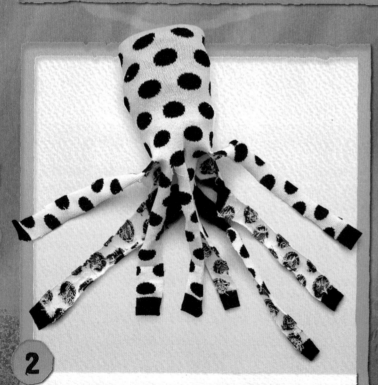

3

Hold a leg and tie it in a knot with the leg that is opposite it. Keep doing this until your octopus stuffing is sealed.

4 Trim the ends of your legs to make points then stick on some googly eyes.

5 Now you can make lots of octopus pals in different colours!

I AM NOT A SOCK...

I'M A FAB FUNNY FACE!

Have fun making these little chaps. Just follow Steps 1-3, then turn your stuffed sock upside down so that the legs become hair. Add some googly eyes, then use a button or a small pompom for the nose. Stitch or glue some wool at the bottom to make a smiley mouth. Who will you create?

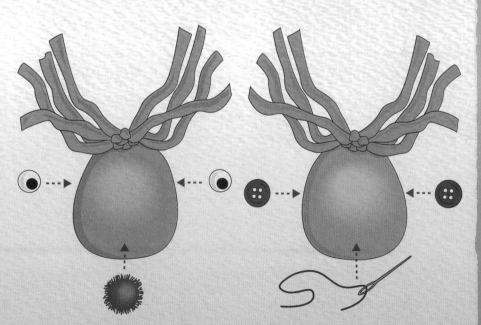

HORSE!

I TROT, CANTER AND GALLOP. WHY? BECAUSE I AM A HORSE, OF COURSE.

DID YOU KNOW? HORSES CAN SLEEP LYING DOWN OR STANDING UP.

YOU WILL NEED

- ONE SOCK
- CARD
- SAFETY SCISSORS
- FABRIC GLUE
- GOOGLY EYES
- WOOL

SET THE SCENE

On a large piece of paper, draw a cosy stable for your horse to snuggle up in. Tear up strips of yellow tissue paper to make hay and doodle some apples for them to snack on, too.

LIVING IN THE **COUNTRYSIDE** IS MUCH BETTER THAN BEING ON A **SMELLY OLD FOOT.**

SOMETIMES I EVEN TAKE **PEOPLE** FOR RIDES ALONG THE **BEACH!**

GO FURTHER!

GRAB A STRIPED SOCK AND HEAD OVER TO THE NEXT PAGE TO MAKE A FABULOUS ZEBRA PUPPET.

NEIGHHHH!

I AM NOT A SOCK...

I'M A HORSE!

1 Cut two small circles out of card and glue them to the toe part of your sock to make nostrils.

2 Next, stick on some googly eyes.

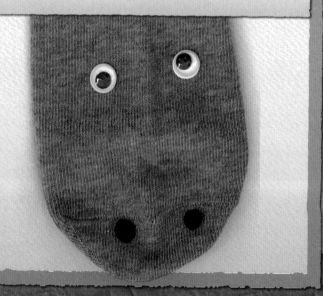

3 Cut two pointy ears out of card, 4cm long by 2cm wide. Cut a smaller shape out of pink paper to make the inside of each ear.

4 Next, tape or glue your ears onto the sock. You might need to put your hand into the sock to help you to see where they need to go.

5 For the mane, cut lengths of wool and glue them between the ears.

I AM NOT A SOCK...

I'M A ZEBRA PUPPET!

All you need to make your zebra puppet is a black and white striped sock. If you don't have one of those, use fabric paint to paint black stripes onto a plain white sock. Now, simply follow the same steps as the horse puppet!

JUGGLING BALLS!

WE ARE A **TEAM** OF **JUGGLING BALLS** OFF TO JOIN THE **CIRCUS!**

TOGETHER WE'RE **TONS OF FUN** AND WE JUST **LOVE** BEING CENTRE STAGE.

YOU WILL NEED
- THREE SOCKS
- TAPE
- THREE HANDFULS OF UNCOOKED RICE

DID YOU KNOW?
THE ANCIENT EGYPTIANS USED TO JUGGLE. A PAINTING OF JUGGLING WAS FOUND IN A TOMB!

SET THE SCENE

Make a stage background for your juggling extravaganza. Just hang some fabric or a colourful bed sheet behind you. You could even design your own circus-style sign and make tickets for your show (just make sure you get some practice in, first!).

CAN YOU KEEP US ALL IN THE AIR?

GO FURTHER!

WE WILL SHOW YOU HOW TO MASTER YOUR JUGGLING SKILLS AND IMPRESS ALL YOUR PALS. TURN OVER THE PAGE TO LET THE FUN BEGIN!

I AM NOT A SOCK...
I'M A SET OF JUGGLING BALLS!

1 Stretch the end of a sock over a reel of sticky tape to keep the sock open. Then add a handful of uncooked rice.

2 Carefully take the sock off the reel of tape and twist the end of sock, like this.

3 Next, put your hand into the sock and pull it through completely. It should now look like this:

4 Again, twist the end of the sock, as you did in Step 2. Put your hand into the sock and repeat Step 3.

5 Keep repeating this step until all of the sock material has been used up and you come to the end of your sock.

6 Your finished juggling ball should look like this from the front and the back. Repeat these steps with different coloured socks to make a set of 3 juggling balls.

I AM NOT A SOCK... **NOW LET'S JUGGLE!** Follow this step-by-step guide to teach yourself how to juggle.

1. Start by throwing one sock high into the air and catching it in your other hand.

2. Now try to throw the ball without looking at it, so that your hand instinctively knows where to go.

3 With one ball in each hand, release one ball to be caught by your opposite hand, then the other.

4. Don't attempt a third ball until you have mastered Step 3! When confident, start with two balls in one hand.

OWL!

TWIT! TWOOO!

I AM A **FEATHERY OWL,** NOT SOME OLD SOCK.

LIVING HIGH UP IN THE TREES, I SPEND MY DAYS SNOOZING AWAY... ZZZZ!

AND THEN WHEN **NIGHT TIME** COMES, I AM **WIDE AWAKE** AND READY FOR **ADVENTURE.**

YOU WILL NEED

- ONE SOCK
- SAFETY SCISSORS
- WADDING
- FABRIC GLUE
- BUTTONS
- ORANGE PAPER OR CARD
- FEATHERS

SET THE SCENE

Make a tree for your owl to perch on by collecting lots of empty cardboard tubes (toilet roll, kitchen roll and wrapping paper tubes work really well!). Paint them brown and tape together to make a tree shape, adding green tissue paper for leaves.

GO FURTHER!

DID YOU KNOW? A GROUP OF OWLS IS CALLED A PARLIAMENT.

WHY STOP AT AN OWL? ON THE NEXT PAGE YOU CAN MAKE A SPOOKY BAT.

I'M AN OWL!

1

Lie your sock flat and snip the ankle part away, so that you're left with the foot section. Next, cut this into a pointy shape, so that it looks like the picture, here:

2

Pop a handful of wadding into your sock and fold over both layers of the pointed part, like this, and glue it in place.

3

Glue on two buttons for eyes and a triangle of orange paper to make the beak.

4

Cut some feet out of orange paper.

5 Glue the feet onto the bottom of your owl.

6 Finally glue feathers to each side of your owl to make the wings.

I AM NOT A SOCK...

I'M A SPOOKY BAT!

To make a bat, use a black sock and follow Steps 1-2. Add googly eyes and fangs cut out of white card. Cut two red or black feet out of card, and glue to the bottom. Finally, make two flapping bat wings out of black card and glue to each side of your bat's body.

CATERPILLAR!

BEING A CATERPILLAR IS THE GREATEST!

I LOVE TO **WRIGGLE UP** YOUR GARDEN PATH AND CHOMP ON **LEAVES** AND **FLOWERS** THAT I PASS.

BUT BEST OF ALL, ONE DAY I'LL TURN INTO A **BUTTERFLY**.

CHOMP! CHOMP!

YOU WILL NEED

- ONE SOCK
- WADDING
- PIPE CLEANERS
- THREAD
- GOOGLY EYES

SET THE SCENE

Make a flower bed for your caterpillar to play in. Simply scrunch up small bits of colourful tissue paper into flower shapes and use a dab of glue to stick them onto a green piece of card. What will your garden look like?

DID YOU KNOW?
A CATERPILLAR HAS OVER 4,000 MUSCLES IN ITS BODY!

GO FURTHER!

ON THE NEXT PAGE, WE WILL SHOW YOU HOW TO MAKE A ROW OF GIANT FLOWERS, USING THE SAME TECHNIQUE AS YOUR CATERPILLAR.

CHOMP!

I'M A CATERPILLAR!

1

For the caterpillar's face, push a handful of wadding into the end of the sock. Then twist a pipe cleaner around it to make a ball shape.

2

Repeat Step 1 to make the rest of the sections of your caterpillar's body, until you have a small section of sock left over.

3

When you get to the end of your sock, make the last section the smallest of all and tie with a piece of thread.

4

Use a pipe cleaner to make the antennae. Bend the middle of the pipe cleaner underneath the head to attach it and then curl each end around a pencil to make a coil.

5

Finally, add a red pipe cleaner for a smiley mouth and stick on two googly eyes.

I AM NOT A SOCK...

I'M A ROW OF FLOWERS!

To make a row of flowers from a sock, just follow Steps 1-4, so that you have a long sock that's divided into sections. These will be the base of your flower bed. Next, cut flower shapes out of colourful paper or card and cut out the centre of the flower so that you are left with the petals. Now slot the petals over the top of each ball. Use a red pen to draw on specks of pollen.

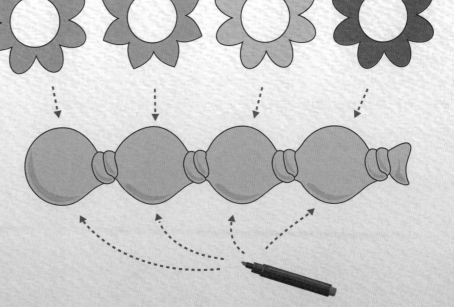

DOG TOY!

I'M A DOG TOY READY TO **PLAY**, AND **TUG OF WAR** IS MY **FAVOURITE** GAME OF ALL.

LET'S PLAY.

DID YOU KNOW?
DOGS CAN SMELL UP TO 10, 000 TIMES BETTER THAN HUMANS CAN.

YOU WILL NEED

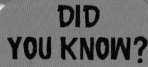

- THREE SOCKS IN DIFFERENT COLOURS

YOU CAN **GIVE ME** TO YOUR DOG AS A **SPECIAL** TREAT WHEN THEY'VE BEEN **EXTRA GOOD.**

WOOF!
WOOF!

GO FURTHER!

IF YOU'VE GOT AN EXTRA SOCK, YOU CAN USE THE SAME TECHNIQUE TO MAKE ANOTHER TOY. TURN THE PAGE TO FIND OUT HOW!

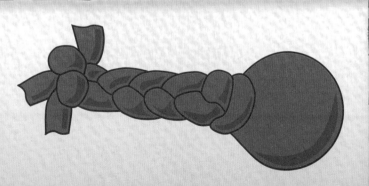

I AM NOT A SOCK...
I'M A DOG TOY!

1 Tie all three socks together at the opening by making a knot, as shown.

2 Now, start to plait the socks together by bringing the right sock into the middle, then the left sock into the middle.

3 Keep going until you reach near the bottom, but leave enough space to tie another knot.

4 Finally, tie a knot in this end of your plait to hold it together.

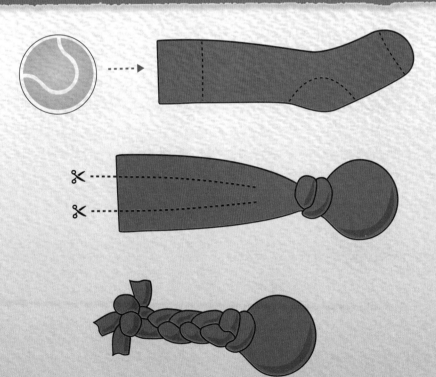

I AM NOT A SOCK...

I'M ANOTHER DOG TOY!

To make a different type of dog toy, put a dog ball into the end of the sock. Tie a big knot to hold it in place, then cut the leftover sock into three strands. Plait these strands and tie another knot in the end and your dog chew is ready! This makes a great toy for playing fetch with, too.

RABBIT!
HOP TO IT...

I HOP ABOUT ALL OVER THE GARDEN AND I STRETCH UP TALL TO GET A GOOD VIEW OF EVERYTHING.

YOU WILL NEED

- ONE SOCK
- TAPE
- UNCOOKED RICE
- THREAD
- SAFETY SCISSORS
- COTTON WOOL
- GOOGLY EYES
- GLUE
- RIBBON

SET THE SCENE

Cut some tasty veggies out of colourful paper for your bunny to munch on. Try orange carrots, or green cabbages and lettuces. Lay them all out in a cardboard box to create a whole vegetable patch!

HAVE YOU SEEN MY CUTE BOB TAIL AND BIG FLOPPY EARS?

IF YOU BRING ME A CARROT, I'LL BE YOUR CHUM FOR LIFE.

GO FURTHER!

DID YOU KNOW?

WHEN RABBITS ARE HAPPY, THEY JUMP INTO THE AIR AND SPIN AROUND.

ONCE YOU'VE MADE ONE RABBIT, WHY NOT USE DIFFERENT SIZED SOCKS TO MAKE A WHOLE BUNNY FAMILY?

I AM NOT A SOCK...
I AM A RABBIT!

1 Stretch the end of your sock over a reel of sticky tape, like this. This makes it easier to fill your sock with uncooked rice.

2 Fill your sock with rice until it is roughly ¾ full. Take out the tape, then tie up the top of the sock tightly with some wool or thread.

3 Then use more thread to make a separate head and body shape, like this. Make sure that the rabbit's head is a little bit smaller than the body.

4 To make the ears, snip the ankle part of the sock in half. Then, trim to make each end pointy.

5 Make a fluffy bob tail from a ball of cotton wool and glue it to the back of your bunny.

6 Stick on googly eyes and stitch a cross to make a mouth. Finish with a sweet ribbon.

I AM NOT A SOCK...

I'M A WHOLE RABBIT FAMILY!

Find different sized socks to make a whole family of rabbits! Use little socks to make some adorable baby bunnies. What will you name them all?

SNAKE!

I AM NOT A SOCK, I AM A SNAKE! YOU'LL KNOW IT'S ME WITH MY SCALES AND LONG FORKED TONGUE.

HISSSS!

SET THE SCENE

Shred green tissue paper to make a grassy bank for your snake to hide in.

YOU WILL NEED

- ONE SOCK
- WADDING
- THREAD
- GOOGLY EYES
- PIPE CLEANER
- TAPE

GO FURTHER!

IF YOU'RE MORE OF A DOG PERSON, THEN YOU CAN MAKE ONE OF THOSE ON THE NEXT PAGE, TOO!

DID YOU KNOW? SNAKES DON'T CHEW THEIR FOOD, THEY SWALLOW IT WHOLE!

I'M THE **CHAMPION** OF **HIDE AND SEEK**... IF WE PLAY IN **LONG GRASS!**

I AM NOT A SOCK...
I'M A SNAKE!

1 Begin stuffing your sock with wadding to make a snake shape.

2 When your sock is stuffed, tie a knot in the end or use thread to keep the stuffing in.

3 Stick on a pair of googly eyes.

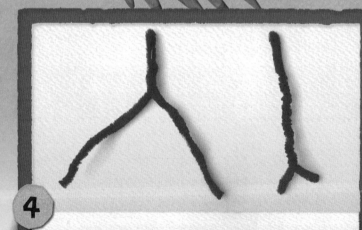

4 Fold a red pipe cleaner in half and twist the ends around each other to make a forked tongue.

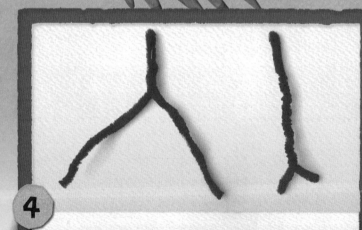

5

Tape the tongue onto the front of your snake.

I AM NOT A SOCK...

I'M A SAUSAGE DOG!

Make the body of your dog by using a brown sock for steps 1-3. Use brown and black card to make ears, a nose and four legs. Tape them to your sausage dog's body. Finally, make a red tongue out of red felt or card.

CAT TOY!

EXCUSE ME, I AM NOT A SOCK. I'M A CAT TOY.

YOU CAN'T CATCH ME.

- ONE SOCK
- WADDING
- SAFETY SCISSORS
- GOOGLY EYES
- GLUE AND TAPE
- STRING

DID YOU KNOW? CATS SLEEP FOR AROUND 16 HOURS EVERY DAY!

BEING **SUPER PLAYFUL** MEANS THAT I CAN KEEP **KITTIES** ON THEIR **TOES** - I MEAN **PAWS!**

GO FURTHER!

KEEP YOUR KITTY SUPER INTERESTED IN THEIR NEW TOY WITH OUR TOP TIPS ON THE NEXT PAGE.

I AM NOT A SOCK...
I'M A CAT TOY!

1

Push a little ball of wadding into the end of a sock.

2

Now tie a knot in the sock to keep the wadding in place.

3

Trim the end of the sock off to make it neat, as shown.

4

You could add a googly eye to make your toy look more like a fish.

5

Next, tape or sew your cat toy to a piece of string ready to play with.

I AM NOT A SOCK...

TOP TIPS!

To make your cat toy even better, tie it to a twig and wiggle it around for your cat to chase after. You could even pop catnip or a treat inside the sock to make your cat super interested!

SNOWMAN!

BEING **FROSTY** AND **ICY COLD** IS MY **FAVOURITE** WAY TO BE, BECAUSE I AM **A SNOWMAN!**

DID YOU KNOW? JAPAN IS THE SNOWIEST PLACE IN THE WORLD.

BRRRR!

BRRRR!

YOU WILL NEED

- ONE WHITE SOCK
- WADDING
- ONE COLOURFUL SOCK
- THREAD
- BUTTONS
- BLACK PEN
- ORANGE PAPER
- GLUE
- SAFETY SCISSORS

I LOVE TO **DRESS UP** IN A BIG **BOBBLE HAT** AND **SCARF.** JUST CHECK OUT MY **COAL EYES** AND **CARROT** NOSE!

42

SET THE SCENE

Make a frosty background scene for your snowman to stand in. Use cotton wool for snow and bits of tin foil for slippery ice. Glue them onto a piece of blue card. Have a go at drawing more snowmen in the picture to keep your snow sock buddy company!

I'M THE SNOWMAN THAT NEVER MELTS!

GO FURTHER!

LET'S MAKE A SOCK PENGUIN TO ADD TO YOUR SNOWY SCENE, TOO. WE WILL SHOW YOU HOW ON THE NEXT PAGE.

I AM NOT A SOCK...
I'M A SNOWMAN!

1

Push wadding into a white sock. Leave enough space so that you can tie a knot in the end.

2

Trim around the knot to neaten it up. Now, make a scarf from a strip of colourful sock and tie it to make a head and body.

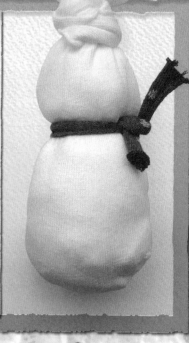

3

Take the rest of the colourful sock and cut the ankle part away like this. Pinch it into a hat shape and tie some thread around it to keep it in place.

4

Now your hat is on, it's time to glue some bright red buttons to the snowman's tummy.

5

Draw on two eyes and a dotty grin using a black pen.

6

Cut a carrot nose out of orange paper and glue it onto your snowman's face.

I AM NOT A SOCK...

I'M A PENGUIN!

Stuff a black sock so that it's around ¾ full and tie a knot in the top. Next, tie a piece of thread around the penguin to make a head and body shape. Cut out round pieces of white fabric (you could use a piece of a white sock) and glue this on to make the penguin's tummy and face. Add googly eyes, tape on a yellow paper beak, and make a hat and scarf from a colourful sock.

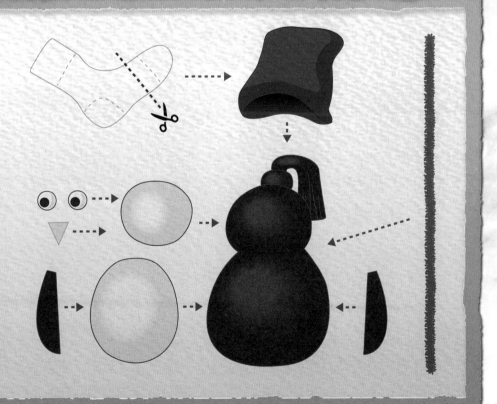

45

YOUR DESIGNS

NOW IT'S OVER TO YOU... THE ONLY THING HOLDING YOUR OLD SOCKS BACK FROM GREATNESS IS YOUR OWN IMAGINATION! SKETCH YOUR IDEAS HERE – WE'VE GIVEN YOU A COUPLE OF OUTLINES TO GET YOU STARTED.

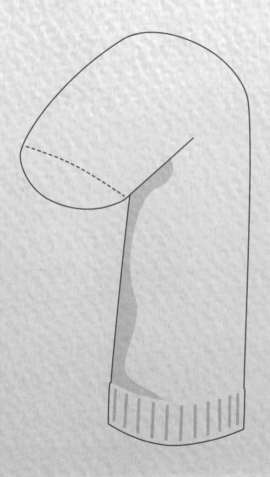
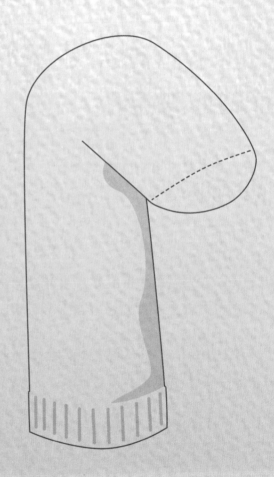

. . . .

owl feet and beaks

horse ears and noses

snowman buttons and noses

rabbit carrots

caterpillar flowers

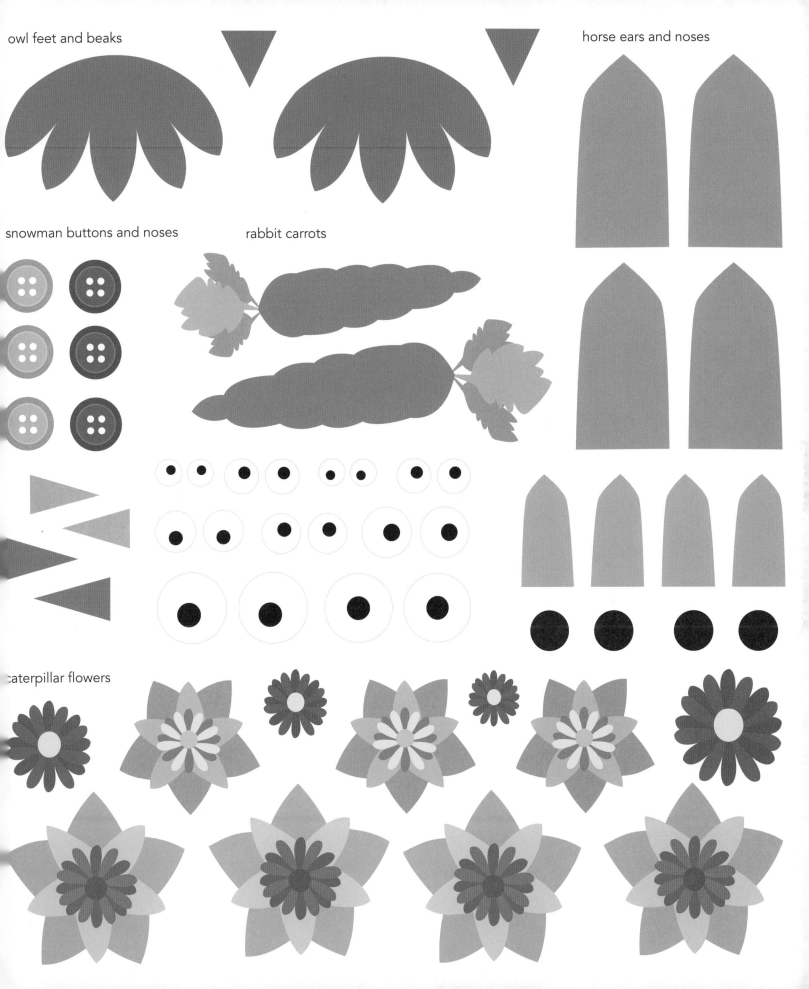